KS2 English

WRITING *FICTION* Test Revision Guide

Pie Corbett & Ann Webley

Badger Publishing

Introduction

This book covers the main different types of fiction writing. It revisits all the types of writing that have been covered in years 3–6. The book would be useful in years 5 and 6 as a way of reviewing text types and preparing for secondary school, as well as preparing for SATs tests. The types of writing covered are:

Each section follows the same pattern:

a **An example of the text type** – this provides a basic example for analysis – how the writing is structured and what features are used.

b **Practice activity 1 and 2** – these activities help to focus on aspects that might need practice or reinforcement.

c **Writing tips** – this page focuses upon thinking about the purpose of the writing and the influence of the audience. It also looks at a simple planning format that can be used to structure ideas.

d **Short tasks** – some tasks to try out. These should take 20 minutes, including planning time.

e **Long tasks** – some tasks to try out. These should take 45 minutes, including planning.

NB: The unit on Planning stories has no text model – but models for planning. There are no writing tasks in this unit.

In my dream I saw
a swift snake silently slip
across the playground bank.

In my dream I heard
the dizzy buzz of bees
busying themselves
in the pale, canary yellow
throat of a daffodil.

In my dream I saw
the white moon,
cold as a bone,
cast crisp shadows.

In my dream I saw
the bright stars like
cold cat's eyes caught
in the headlights.

In my dream I heard
the winter wind
muttering to itself,
gossiping with
the restless grass.

In my dream I saw
the red-faced sun,
struggle over the horizon,
casting nets of light,
tugging my silver self
up from sleep
like a salmon
from the deep.

Pie Corbett

Using well-chosen words

Improve these sentences by changing the 'weak' words:

1 The nice moon shone on the nice mountains.
2 The horrid man looked at the horrid dog.
3 The big branches on the big tree looked like big fingers.
4 The thin snake was as thin as can be.
5 The man got out of the car and went into the shop.
6 The old woman went slowly to the counter and spoke quietly.

Using alliteration

Write alliterative sentences about these animals:

cat   tarantula   scorpion   shark   cobra   wasp

For instance:

The curious cat calmly crept by the cool canal.

Using onomatopoeia

Write sentences using these words, in which you use onomatopoeia:

snake   waves   thunder   brakes   bell   fire alarm

For instance :

The snake spat and hissed.

Using a simile to build a picture

Complete these similes with new ideas:

- as quick as (not a cheetah!)
- as hot as (not the sun or an oven)
- as slow as (not a snail)
- the stars are like...
- the moon is like...
- the clouds are like...
- a leaf looks like...

Using personification and metaphor to build a picture

Complete these sentences by using personification, e.g. The tree stooped, bending its back.

The rain...
The wind...
The lightning...
The thunder...
The snow...

WRITING TIPS

Tackling the writing

▶ Concentrate on the subject when writing – try to see it in your mind.

▶ Brainstorm words, ideas, phrases.

▶ Select from the brainstorm – and discard – to build up the poem.

▶ Poetry is about quality not quantity.

▶ Keep saying the poem to yourself as you are writing, to check if it 'sounds right', if it flows.

▶ Try out unusual and inventive combinations – struggle to seek the new – do not be content with the first idea – always sift through other words and select the one that gives the most impact.

▶ Use the line breaks to emphasise words or a phrase, to help the reader and to give the poem a shape.

Select words with care

▶ Create strong pictures by using **similes**, **metaphors** and **personification**.

▶ Create memorable sounds by using **repetition** for effect, **alliteration**, **onomatopoeia**, **rhythm** and **rhyme**.

▶ Do not be lazy when using similes – try to create something new.

▶ Create powerful poems by choosing:
   • precise nouns (*Siamese* not *cat*)
   • powerful verbs (*whisper* not *said*)
   • adjectives that add something 'new' to the noun – look for something a little unusual that helps to describe – build up the picture
   • words that do not obviously go together so that you surprise the reader, e.g. Not '*the old lady hobbled down the road*' but try '*the old lady break-danced*'!

▶ When using adverbs, make sure that the verb is powerful enough (*walked slowly* or *ambled*?).

▶ Avoid repeating a word unless you need to for effect.

- ▶ Do not use the first word that occurs to you – think!
- ▶ Avoid overwriting - especially using too many adjectives or adverbs.
- ▶ Forcing a rhyme can lead to dishonest writing. Go for the right word rather than a forced rhyme.
- ▶ Keep the writing concrete and detailed.

SHORT TASKS

1 Write an animal counting poem from one to ten that uses alliteration in every line, e.g.

> *One white wombat worried with a weak worm.*
>
> *Two trembling tortoises took... etc.*

2 Write an eight line poem using personification in each line. The sentences are started for you – and the first is completed.

Outside the classroom window –

The trees twiddle their thumbs and wait patiently.

The fence...

The grass...

The playground...

The clouds...

The sun...

The street light...

The cars...

LONG TASKS

1 Write a poem about a magical window. Through the window you can see anything! Use a repeating sentence starter, e.g. *Through the magic window I saw...*

In the poem use examples of: well-chosen words, alliteration, simile ('like' and 'as'), personification and metaphor, e.g.

> *Through the magic window I saw*
> *The pink dawn crack open the night.*

> *Through the magic window I saw*
> *A blue bus blundering down the silent streets.*

2 Write a poem about the five senses. Use a simple pattern, e.g.

I saw...

I touched...

I tasted...

I heard...

I smelled...

Make each line special by selecting words with care to create surprise and contrasts. You must use examples of: simile ('like' and 'as'), alliteration, personification, metaphor, e.g.

> *I saw a cold sun*
> *Glint like a fish's scale*
> *Flickering between dark clouds.*

2

Description

A place

One of my favourite secret places is at my Grandad's house. There is an old shed at the bottom of the field and I don't think that anyone else goes there.

It is dark inside and it takes quite a time for your eyes to get accustomed to the faint light. The windows are grimy. Dust covers everything in a fine layer like talcum powder. Don't blow – or you'll sneeze. It is damp there and smells of oil. Spectacular cobwebs hang like fine curtains, draped lace clogged with dust.

There is a long workbench covered in old tools – a claw hammer, a monkey wrench and rusty nails lie scattered. At the back of the shed is an old tarpaulin thrown over a motorbike. The paint is peeling and the wheels are locked. Time has scratched scars on its once gleaming body.

It is a place trapped in the past. Only the spiders and I know of its secret.

A person

My Great Aunt Mabel is probably the most unusual person that I have met. In fact, she is so extraordinary that if I describe her I do not expect you to believe me.

She is over ninety now. Her back is so hunched that she cannot stand up straight any longer. She walks along, stooped like a question mark or Sherlock Holmes always looking for that elusive clue. She likes to wear a thin, plastic Macintosh – light blue usually. On her feet she wears rubber shoes called galoshes. These are enormous, black and shiny. They are so large because she used to be a dancer and was told that tight shoes could ruin your feet.

Her hair is pure white. It used to be brown but when we were out walking one day she stepped into a bee swarm and had to go to hospital to have the stings removed. When I next saw her, her hair was white.

She speaks in a low, slow gravelly voice. Her skin on her hands is a surprise – cold, thin and wrinkled. You can see a network of tiny blue veins. Her eyes are milky. The skin sags around them so she looks at you like a sad old bulldog. One that I will never forget.

An object

I suppose that everyone has a few keepsakes. By my bed I have a special box that contains all my treasure.

The box came from India — but I bought it in Birmingham! It is painted on the outside — a shiny brown. It has some strange, white birds painted on top. I think of it as my bird box. It has a brass latch that keeps it shut. If you flick the latch the lid springs up, to reveal 4 drawers. Each one has a carved design — a pattern of flowers and what looks like vine leaves weaving round the border.

When the drawers are open you can smell India! It is a rich, mysterious smell — a mixture of seasoned wood, incense and a wildness that I cannot name. Sometimes at night I lie in bed holding the box, feeling its smooth surface, the sharp corners and cold latch. What secrets it could tell…

An event

I love going to the school fair. It is held every year in the school hall.

The stalls are packed around the side of the hall and down the middle. Each stall is piled high with all the things that we have been bringing in for the past few weeks. Mountains of discarded clothes spill off the jumble stall. Old shirts with no collars, bright pink jumpers that no one would be seen DEAD in, leather boots, odd socks and a suit that looks as if it had been made a thousand years ago.

The hall is full of jostling people. Grandparents who usually stand calmly at the bus stop suddenly become like rugby players – barging and pushing to get what they want. The cake stall is cleared in a matter of minutes.

The toy stall has all our cast-offs. Old Barbie dolls with a missing limb, My Little Pony that has had the hair pulled out and mutilated Pokemon. I usually end up buying back what I donated. For some reason I found it hard to say goodbye to my toys!

Descriptions rely on you using your senses. Look at this sentence which has three parts to it.

I saw his shuffling walk, the crumpled coat and torn shirt.

Now write sentences with the same pattern of three, using the sentence starters given below.

Describing a place

I stared at the...

I heard the...

Describing a person

I looked at...

I watched...

Using similes

Now invent similes to help build description.

His hair was like...

His nails were sharp as...

Her teeth were like...

Her fists were like...

His eyes looked like...

Building a description

Take something that you can see, e.g. a gate.

Now add in an adjective, e.g. a rusty gate.

Now make it do something, e.g.

A rusty gate creaks in the wind.

Think of a place that you know well. Make notes in answer to these questions. Then use the notes to create a description, building on the ideas.

1 Write down what you can see there. Add in descriptive words and similes.

2 Write down what you can smell.

3 Write down what you can hear.

4 Write down what things feel like when you touch them.

5 What does it remind you of?

6 How do you feel when you are there?

7 What do you do there?

WRITING TIPS

Tackling the writing

▶ Look carefully at what you are describing.

▶ Try to see it in your mind.

▶ Look carefully for details.

▶ Use all your senses – what does it look like, feel like, smell like…

▶ Be precise, concrete and detailed.

▶ It can help to jot down what you can see and then build words around your first ideas. For instance, when describing a place you might see clouds, trees, fence, etc. Now take these words and build around each one, adding in more detail, e.g. dreary clouds drift across the sky, winter trees sketch a pattern against the sky, the broken fence crumbles.

Select words with care

▶ Create strong pictures by using similes, metaphors and personification.

▶ Do not be lazy when using similes – try to create something new.

▶ Create memorable sounds by using alliteration, onomatopoeia.

▶ Create powerful descriptions by choosing:
- precise nouns (*terrier* not *dog*)
- powerful verbs (*mumbled* not *said*)
- adjectives that add something 'new' to the noun – look for something a little unusual that helps to describe – build up the picture
- words that do not obviously go together so that you surprise the reader, e.g. Not '*the baby crawled*' but try '*the baby tap danced*'!

▶ When using adverbs, make sure that the verb is powerful enough (*talked quietly* or *whispered*?).

▶ Avoid repeating a word unless you need to for effect.

▶ Do not use the first word that occurs to you – think!

▶ Avoid overwriting – especially using too many adjectives or adverbs.

SHORT TASKS

1 Look carefully at this picture of an old man. Write a description of a person like this in only two or three paragraphs. You can base it on the picture or someone that you know. You can invent detail if you like. Think about the following:
- physical details, e.g. his face, mouth, eyes, etc;
- how he speaks – typical things he says;
- how he walks;
- clothes;
- typical things he does.

2 Write a brief description in two or three paragraphs about a place where you have spent a memorable holiday or a memorable visit / trip. Think about the following:
- where is this place;
- what you can see there – include detail;
- what happens there;
- what you can hear;
- explain why it is memorable.

LONG TASKS

1 Write a letter to a relative describing a recent event that made an impression on you. This might have been something that happened in school, on holiday, or at home. Make the description vivid so that your relative can imagine what it was like to be there. Include in your description:
- an explanation about the event;
- a description of what happened;
- what you saw and heard;
- why this was so memorable.

2 Something of great value has been stolen. You have to write a description of this precious object for the police. (You can invent the object or select from the illustration below and invent details). Include:
- what it is and why it is precious;
- what it looks like;
- describe details such as shape, size, colour;
- what it feels like;
- include plenty of detail;
- what is it used for;
- where it was last seen.

3

Planning Stories

The 'Story Mountain'

All stories are based on this basic pattern.

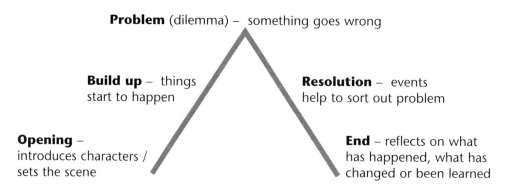

Problem (dilemma) – something goes wrong

Build up – things start to happen

Resolution – events help to sort out problem

Opening – introduces characters / sets the scene

End – reflects on what has happened, what has changed or been learned

Opening	introduces the characters and sets the initial scene.
Build up	the action begins – the characters do something.
Problem (dilemma)	something goes wrong – mystery or dramatic incident that needs sorting out.
Resolution	a series of events help to solve the problem.
Ending	the tale is rounded off, usually revealing what the characters have learned or gained from what has happened.

You can use this pattern to plan a simple 5 part story. There are many different patterns based on this idea, e.g.

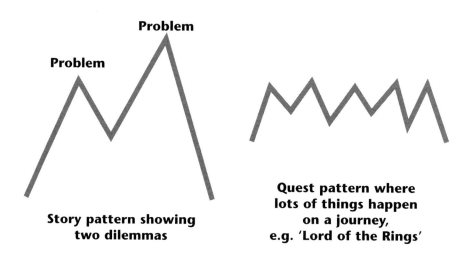

Story pattern showing two dilemmas

Quest pattern where lots of things happen on a journey, e.g. 'Lord of the Rings'

Getting ideas for your story

Always be on the lookout for a story idea. You can borrow ideas:
- listen out for what people say;
- pick up ideas from real events;
- keep an eye on the news for unusual stories;
- turn jokes into stories;
- take a well-known story and alter it;
- retell a fairy tale from a modern viewpoint;
- keep a notebook for ideas.

Using a story map

Draw a map to help plan a quest story. Think about:
- Who is your main character?
- Do they have a companion?
- What is their task?
- Where does the journey start and end?
- What will they meet en route?
- Draw the details onto the story map.

Using a flow chart

Write each scene or paragraph into each box of a flow chart. Keep the tale simple – it can help to jot down possible paragraph starters, e.g.

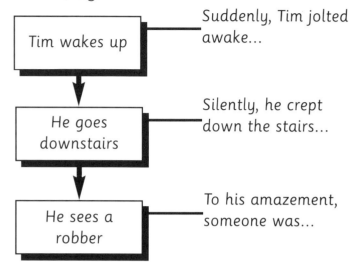

Using a paragraph grid

This can act as a useful paragraph planner. Though when writing you may find that what you thought was going to take one paragraph actually needs more. Also – a planned ending does give direction to your story but you may get a better idea as you near the end.

Tim is told <u>not</u> to go swimming.	He decides to go swimming.	He cannot get out of the water.
A dog saves him.	He goes home soaking wet.	His mum tells him off!

Four basic questions

Use these questions to help you think through a few basics – every time you set out to write a story. It also helps to make a note of your opening and ending line.

Who
- Your main character is crucial.
- Avoid having too many characters.
- Keep the same character for several stories.
- Decide on the name, a few details and the sort of person they are.
- Have contrasting characters as this will lead to conflict.
- Think of a goodie and a baddie!

Where
- Where will the story start?
- Where do the characters go?
- Where does it end?
- Decide on atmospheric places for suspense.
- Think of details to bring settings alive.
- What can you see and hear?

When
- Is this set in the past or present?
- Is this an 'I' story or 'she/he'?

What
- Decide on how to get the tale going.
- What will be the main problem?
- How could it be sorted out?
- How might the tale end?

Four basic plots

1 A warning story

- characters are warned not to do something;
- they do it;
- it goes wrong;
- they have to be rescued.

2 A suspense tale

- characters are doing something;
- it is all going well;
- they see/hear something suspicious;
- they get chased;
- they run/hide;
- they get away.

3 A lost story

- character is sent out to do something;
- walks somewhere;
- gets lost;
- wanders around;
- finds way out/is found.

4 A quest story

- character is given a task;
- sets off;
- things go wrong on the journey;
- reaches end of journey;
- completes task.

1 Map well-known stories onto the story mountain, drawing the graph of what happens.

2 Take a well-known nursery rhyme and put the scenes into a flow chart, e.g.

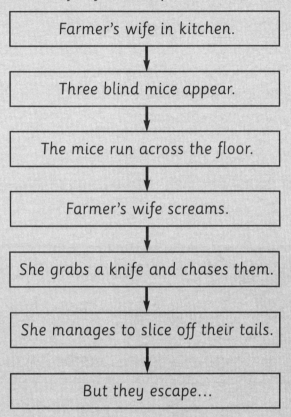

```
┌─────────────────────────────────┐
│     Farmer's wife in kitchen.    │
└─────────────────────────────────┘
                 │
                 ▼
┌─────────────────────────────────┐
│      Three blind mice appear.    │
└─────────────────────────────────┘
                 │
                 ▼
┌─────────────────────────────────┐
│   The mice run across the floor. │
└─────────────────────────────────┘
                 │
                 ▼
┌─────────────────────────────────┐
│      Farmer's wife screams.      │
└─────────────────────────────────┘
                 │
                 ▼
┌─────────────────────────────────┐
│  She grabs a knife and chases them. │
└─────────────────────────────────┘
                 │
                 ▼
┌─────────────────────────────────┐
│ She manages to slice off their tails. │
└─────────────────────────────────┘
                 │
                 ▼
┌─────────────────────────────────┐
│        But they escape...        │
└─────────────────────────────────┘
```

3 Practice inventing problems for stories. What might go wrong in these situations:
   • Two boys go fishing.
   • Tina buys a new computer.
   • A hobbit crosses the mountains to see friends.
   • The new school library is going to be opened by a pop star.

4 Start a class collection of possible names for characters and settings.

5 Map simple tales from well-known picture books onto a flow chart or story mountain. Try changing the names and setting, and add in more events to make the story your own.

6 Take a fairy tale that you know well and modernise it. Rewrite it from another viewpoint, set in your locality.

The opening

Jodie barged her way into the classroom. She stood for a moment by the door and then decided. Dashing across the room, she sat down at the computer. She only had a few minutes and then everyone would be back in from break-time. She grabbed Sandy's bag and began to search frantically. Where on earth was it?

A cough from the door interrupted her...

The ending

Jodie picked up the bag and began the long journey back to her mum's. The street-lights were flickering on and the cold winter's evening was emptying the streets. As she turned the corner into Grafton Street, Jodie heard someone shout and Sandy dashed up to join her. He grinned and handed her a slice of chocolate. They walked on in silence. Being in class 13 would never be the same again. And they both knew it.

Introducing characterisation

Mrs Jenkins turned to look at her son. She shook her head and tutted. His hair was unbrushed, his shirt untucked and there was mud on his trousers. He looked as if he had been for a cross-country walk.

Alfie glared back at his Mum. His fists were still bunched and his heart pounded. They had almost caught him and he did not want to think about what would have happened if they had.

"Leave me be," Alfie snapped, before his mother had had time to say anything. He turned and stomped his way up to his room. He needed to be alone.

Mrs Jenkins listened as he thumped his way upstairs and wondered what could have caused such a mood. He'd been acting strangely for the past week…

Breaking up the dialogue

"Come on," bellowed Maggot, grabbing the rope swing and leaping off the wall. Misha spun round and stared in amazement. He had actually done it! She watched him swish out, swing across the stream and leap onto the opposite bank. Now it's my turn, she thought. In the distance she could hear the hounds barking.

"OK," Misha shouted, as she jumped up onto the wall and grabbed the rope.

Creating a fantasy setting

Jalwar sat down at the table. To his amazement one of the plates began to move towards him. It was being drawn by two miniature elephants, like a small horse-drawn carriage. Then a tiny giraffe trotted across the white linen and poured a black liquid into a green goblet.

Out of the window, he could see the suns setting. Already the orange moon was casting its soft light. The Banyan trees curled up and began to gently snore…

Varying sentences

When writing stories you need to vary your sentences to create different effects. Imitate these sentence types, look out for them in your reading and use them in your writing. For instance:

Short sentences give dramatic effect, e.g.

They were trapped by the ogre.

Exclamations are good for impact, e.g.

"Run!"

Questions draw the reader in, e.g.

Which door should they open?

Compound sentences are useful to keep the writing flowing (and, but, so), e.g.

They ran down the corridor <u>and</u> into the room at the end.

Complex sentences allow you to add in extra layers of information / action, e.g.

While the ogre busied herself with the cooking pot, Skater hid behind a pepper pot.

A sentence of three can help to pile up action, e.g.

Skater turned the lid, climbed into the pot and hid.

Varying the opening of a sentence

A sentence that starts with an 'ing' clause can add variety, e.g.

Mutter<u>ing</u> to herself, the ogre picked up the pepper pot.

A sentence that starts with an 'ed' clause can add variety, e.g.

Surpris<u>ed</u> by the sudden movement, Skater sat up.

A sentence that starts with an adverb emphasises how something happened, e.g.

<u>Cautiously</u>, he peeped out of the pot.

A sentence that starts with 'but' can add emphasis, e.g.

<u>But</u> the ogre saw him.

Dropping in clauses

Look at this basic sentence:

Skater ran across the playground.

You can 'drop' a clause into the sentence to add in more information. Look at these three types (a 'who' clause, an 'ing' and an 'ed' clause) and imitate them, inventing your own. Notice how the commas mark off the clause.

Skater, who was exhausted, ran across the playground.

Skater, trembling with fear, ran across the playground.

Skater, terrified by the ogre's laugh, ran across the playground.

Using connectives

Connectives are very handy because they help you to add in extra information to a sentence. They create links between ideas, between sentences and between paragraphs. Imitate the sentences, using the connectives and following the pattern. Notice where the comma comes.

After the ogre had eaten its supper, it lay down and slept.

As the phoenix flew higher, Skater gripped on.

Because the wind was freezing, Maggot tugged the fur coat closer to him.

Before the ogre returned, Skater found the golden charm.

While the fire started to roar, Skater sneaked towards the door.

Starting paragraphs

In story writing you begin a new paragraph for various different reasons, e.g.

• change of time

Early the next morning, that afternoon, later on that day, as soon as, while, when, after, before, that night, the next day, a month later...

• change of place

On the other side of the road, across the valley...

• change of person

Frank walked in, Francis screamed...

• change of event

The dog bounded up, a car screeched round the corner...

• new speaker

"Hello," said Sally.

• dramatic event, interrupting action

A scream shattered the silence...

• thoughts in the head

Sal knew what it meant...

Read through any novel that you have to hand. Collect useful connectives or sentence starts that are used to open paragraphs. List them under the different headings – and use them in your own writing!

WRITING TIPS

Story openings

▶ You can begin by setting the scene to create atmosphere;

▶ or by introducing your main character;

▶ or with an exciting incident;

▶ or by hinting that something might be about to happen.

Strategies for the opening line

▶ Use **dialogue** – *"Watch out," snapped Billy…*

▶ Use **time** – *One wintry evening…*

▶ Use a **question** – *"What is that?" asked the caretaker…*

▶ Introduce something **intriguing** – *Billy picked up the gas mask…*

▶ Give a **warning** – *"Don't go to the canal," snapped Miss Turner…*

▶ Introduce the **monster** – *Billy thought that ghosts did not exist…*

Techniques for introducing characters

▶ Use an interesting name, e.g. *Maggot Gibson.*

▶ Limit description to one or two details.

▶ Show how the character feels, e.g. *sad, lonely, angry.*

▶ Show what type of person they are, e.g. *bossy, shy.*

▶ Use powerful verbs to show how a character feels and behaves, e.g. *muttered, ambled.*

▶ Rely on portraying character through action and dialogue.

▶ Reveal the reactions of other characters – have them gossiping about the main character.

▶ Reveal the thoughts in the head of the main character.

▶ Base story characters on people you know – and invent a bit!

▶ Keep thinking as you write – what would this person say or do now?

WRITING TIPS

Techniques for creating the setting

▶ Use detail to make settings seem real – sense impressions – what can be seen, heard, smelt, touched or tasted.

▶ Base settings on places that you know plus some invented detail. If you know the place then you will be able to see it in your mind's eye – and pick out detail to bring it alive.

▶ Use real or invented names to bring places alive - to help make the setting more real and believable.

▶ Create atmosphere, e.g. think about what might be hidden, what is dangerous, what looks unusual, what is out of place in your setting.

▶ Use a precise place, the weather, time of day and season to create atmosphere.

Resolution and ending

Techniques for resolving the dilemma:

▶ Make the character(s) do something unexpected.

▶ Have a 'helper' in the story – a Gandalf type who appears and bales the main character out.

▶ Have someone who has been unfriendly suddenly 'do the right thing'.

▶ Show that the problem/dilemma was only in the character's mind and not real.

▶ Allow the character some extra effort to overcome the problem – a sudden superhuman effort.

▶ Only resolve a part of the dilemma so the character learns a lesson for the future.

Possible options for ending a story:

▶ Show how a character has changed.

▶ Show what a character has learned.

▶ Have the main character resolve never to do something again.

▶ Use dialogue – a comment from one of the characters about what has happened.

▶ Avoid clichéd endings – and do not rush it!

SHORT TASKS

1 Write two or three paragraphs that open a story, introducing an angry character. Think about what happens as a result of the character being angry. How do others react? Make sure that you show your character is angry through what they say, do and think.

2 Write half a page of dialogue between two characters. One is bossy and the other is shy. One is trying to get the other one to do something silly. You do not have to have them say much – remember to build up the picture for the reader, so that they can picture:
• what the speaker is doing;
• what the listener is doing;
• the background;
• you might also reveal what characters are thinking or feeling.
Do not write a string of speech.

3 Write the final paragraph to a story that began with one of these opening lines:
• *Chapman was lonely.*
• *Harflight, the dwarf, stared at the map.*
• *Elliot picked up the stone, closed his eyes and threw it.*
• *The quarry was a dangerous place.*

4 Write two or three paragraphs that involve a fantasy setting. Remember to describe detail, to add inventive touches and create the scene by describing what can be seen and heard.

LONG TASKS

1 Write a story that starts in a school, titled '*The Warning*'.
2 Write a story that starts at home, titled '*In trouble again*'.
3 Write a story that begins with these words, '*Fraser had wanted a gameboy for over a year...*'
4 Write a story that ends with the words, '*Kim shook her head. She would never be that stupid again.*'

5

Traditional Tales

Once, in faraway times, there lived a wise King, beloved by all his subjects. Now, this King was growing old and he worried about the future of his Kingdom – for his only son, whom he loved dearly, took no notice of affairs of state and spent all his time reading books.

One day, he decided to set the Prince a task to see if he was fit to rule the country. Kings can do this if they wish. Summoning the boy to the Royal Throne Room he said, "My son, I wish you to leave your beloved books for just one month and travel our realm to bring back the three most precious things in the world."

The studious Prince had no idea why his father should make such a strange request but set off without further ado. As he rode along the dusty track out of the city, he wondered what he should look for. Would he find gold? Should he bring jewels? Surely these things would please his father. But three things?

So he journeyed on, puzzling as he went and soon entered a deep, dark forest. There, lying beside the tallest tree, was a dirty, ragged child. "What is the matter, little boy?" the Prince asked.

The boy looked up. "A gang stole my knapsack. I've had no food for two days," he replied.

The Prince did not hesitate. "Share my food," he said and handed over some wonderful delicacies from the Royal Kitchen. The boy ate gratefully and, as he did so, a glow appeared around his head. The Prince thought nothing of it.

"Here," said the boy, "take this for your generosity." And he handed the Prince a blue bottle, bubbling with warmth and promise. The studious Prince had seen nothing like it before, but thanked the boy and went on his way.

Days later, still worrying about what to bring back to his father, the Prince rode into a small town, hoping to find a comfortable bed for the night. In the square, two groups of men were fighting while townsfolk ranged on either side, shouting support to one or the other.

"What is going on?" the young Prince asked.

"It's the council," a woman told him. "If they can't agree, they sort it out by fighting. It's always been the same. We hate it. But what can we do?"

The Prince did not hesitate. He stepped into the middle of the brawl and held up his hands. The town square fell silent. "You cannot run your town like this," he said. "Listen to me." So the Prince told them a story from one of his books about a Kingdom where people made decisions among themselves without violence. It was as though a veil had lifted from their eyes.

"Why didn't we think of this before!" cried the mayor. As he spoke, a glow appeared around his head. The Prince thought nothing of it. "Here, take this for showing us fairness," the mayor continued and handed the Prince a red bottle, bubbling with warmth and promise. The studious Prince had seen nothing like it before, but thanked the mayor and went on his way.

The month had nearly passed and still the young Prince had not found the three most precious things in the world. He was so deep in thought that he almost failed to notice a young girl beside the road. She was an ugly thing and she was crying. The Prince got off his horse and went over to her.

"What is the matter, young maid? Why do you cry?"

"All the girls in my village laugh at me," she explained. "They say I am ugly and that I will never be kissed."

The Prince did not hesitate. He bent towards her and kissed the pock-marked face. As he did so, a glow appeared around her head. The Prince thought nothing of it.

The girl smiled and handed him a yellow bottle, bubbling with warmth and promise. "Here," she said, "take this for making me so happy." The studious Prince had seen nothing like it before, but thanked the girl and turned for home.

"I'm sorry, father," he said, when at last he reached the Royal Throne Room. "I failed you. I have not found the three most precious things in the world. I have used up all my provisions and have only these three bottles left."

The King held out his hand and took the bottles and as soon as he saw them, he knew what had happened. Some Kings are very wise. So he uncorked the bottles, bubbling with warmth and magic, and watched as his Kingdom was flooded with plenty, with peace and with love. And he knew that his son would one day make a very good King.

Useful sentences

These sentences are in the style used in traditional tales. Try completing them in different ways. Work with a partner or in a group.

Some sentences are useful at the beginning:

Once upon a time there lived...

Long ago, in a... there lived... who ...

In long ago times, ...

Once, in faraway times, ...

In a forest lived...

Once there was a wicked King...

Other sentences help to link parts of the story together:

One particular day, ...

Time passed and the old man...

So the young man...

Next morning, the King...

Some sentences help to give the author's voice:

And so, from that day to this, ...

You can imagine what happened next, can't you? ...

Of course...

Tell a story

Traditional tales were told aloud.

Try doing this in your group. One of you can begin with one of the starts you have just been practising. When one person stops, the next takes over. You will have to listen very hard to pick up clues for the plot. Have fun!

Agony Aunt

"I want you to go to the market today, Tom," said his mother. "We have almost no money left so you must take some vegetables to sell."

"OK. I'll go," the boy replied. He set off down the road and soon came to the market.

This was supposed to be the introduction to a traditional tale but the author hasn't got the style quite right.

Write some advice using the check list for writing in your classroom.

Then have a go at re-writing it yourself!

Quick planning games

Work in pairs on quick planning ideas. Can you think of an idea for a tale in 5 minutes?!

Here are some starter words to get you going:

- a lonely girl, an old woman, a piece of magic fruit;

- a poor woman, a strange visitor, a bottomless pot;

- a King, three sons, a journey;

- a poor farmer, 3 wishes, an evil princess.

WRITING TIPS

- ▶ To write in the style of a traditional tale you need to include the right sort of elements.

- ▶ Use stock characters – king, queen, prince, princess, poor miller, farmer, beggar woman, 3 brothers or sisters, a giant.

- ▶ Characters are not well described and are simplistic, e.g. a good king.

- ▶ Use creatures – hare, rabbit, tortoise, spider, fox, wolf, bear, coyote.

- ▶ Use stock settings – forest, palace, tower, lake, path, crossroads, cottage. No elaborate description is needed.

- ▶ Use typical objects, e.g. a spinning wheel, a mirror, a porridge pot, a stone, a sack, axes, a pot of gold, a comb, a house on chicken legs.

- ▶ Use typical events – being granted 3 wishes, setting out on a journey.

- ▶ Use typical language, especially connectives, e.g. *once, not twice, but once upon a time, in the land where east meets west, far away…*

- ▶ Stick to the bare bones of the telling – traditional tales do not loiter on description but are driven by what happened next.

- ▶ Have simple themes – good over evil, simple beats clever, poor versus rich, kind versus cruel, greed versus generosity.

- ▶ Use the power of three – three characters, the same thing happens three times, repeating a catchy sentence 3 times.

- ▶ Rhythmic and musical repetitions can enhance the telling.

- ▶ The good triumph over evil by the end.

1 THE UNHAPPY PRINCESS

Use this picture to write the introduction and next paragraph of a traditional tale.

2 THE MAGIC FOREST

This is a section from the middle of the story:

Time passed and the young girl walked deeper into the wood. She pulled her cloak tightly around her because of the wind and gripped the handle of her little basket.

Presently, she met a rabbit on the path and was not, by now, at all astonished to hear an animal speak.

Write the next section of the story. Think about where the girl may be going and why and what the animal is going to do to help.

LONG TASKS

1 STORY SOUP

Look at the following two lists. Choose 2 or 3 characters, a setting and an object. Then mix the ingredients together – plan and write a traditional tale. Don't forget to use all the features you have been practising.

Settings: inside a poor house, outside a palace, a wood, a bridge by a stream, a ring of stones.

Objects: a pile of sticks, a magic pot, a string of pearls, a mirror, a basket of food, a lamp, a chest of gold.

2 THE QUEST

Write a traditional story that features a sad princess. In the story the King offers a reward to anyone who can make her laugh.

6

Adventure Stories

Sam had just closed his eyes. The train rattled on through the night and he was weary. He could hear the lady, who had been sitting opposite him, fumbling with something. Then she spoke.

"I can talk now. There's only a kid and he's asleep. I'll throw the package off just before Kingsnorth station as we agreed. And you'd better pay good." She snapped the phone shut. Sam lay quite still, trying to let his breathing sound slow and steady. His heart seemed to be thumping so loud that he was amazed that she couldn't hear it.

At that moment, he heard her get up, open the door and then the carriage was empty. He opened one eye, then the other. She had left her stuff behind on the seat – a leather bag and a small package, tightly wrapped up in black plastic.

Sam stared at the package transfixed. It came to him in a moment. He had heard it on the news at his aunt's house before he had got onto the train. The sultan of Bronay had been robbed of his crown jewels. It seemed impossible but Sam realised that he might be sitting opposite what half the police force in the country were looking for.

Without thinking, he grabbed the package and ducked out into the corridor. It was deserted. Which way to run? He decided to head for the back of the train. Locking himself into a toilet, he waited till the next station.

Twenty minutes later Sam jumped down onto a lonely, dark platform. He was in the middle of nowhere. He had no time to look about him for as soon as he left the train, the lady stuck her head out of a window and began shouting. Sam ran.

He dashed over the railway bridge and out onto a town high street. From up the street a car left the side of the road and began to drive towards him. Faster. Faster. Too fast. Its engines revved angrily and Sam knew that if he didn't move quickly he was looking at his final moments. For a second his legs seemed paralised, rooted to the spot with fear. Just as the car's angry, yellow eyes seemed to have him trapped, he leaped onto the bank and it shot past, brakes screeching.

Sam didn't wait to look back. Clutching the package, he turned and ran up the bank. Scrambling over the fence, he found himself running across an allotment. He could hear the men shouting and knew that they were following him. But he had a good start.

Ten minutes later he climbed the fence the other side. He was looking out across a sandy beach down into the sea. Along the beach stood a row of huts. In the moonlight they looked like strange guard boxes. Sam looked over his shoulder but could no longer see the men. They had wandered to the wrong side and had lost his trail, stumbling about in the darkness.

Sam trotted down to the row of huts. He walked along, trying each door till he found one that was unlocked. Inside was a small table, a few deck chairs and, to his relief, a rug. He tugged the door to, blocked it with the table and lay down on the floor with the rug over him.

When he awoke, sunlight filtered through the wooden beach hut. Sam sat up. He stared at the package, wondering what the contents looked like. He was reluctant to open it – supposing it was the lady's sandwiches – what then? Besides, he had to get in touch with his Mum. She'd be worried sick by now.

Sam crept out of the hut, peering up and down the beach. There was no one in sight. Just the odd seagull and the sound of the waves pummeling the beach below him. Cautiously, he wandered along the sea front into the town. He kept pausing, his eyes scanning for the two men. In the end he found a phone box and managed to get through to his Mum.

"You wait where you are," was all that she said. Brisk and to the point. He knew that she would sort it out. He stood in the phone box, watching the early morning traffic trundle by. At that moment, the door flew open and Sam stared in dismay. He recognised the men immediately.

"We'll have that," snapped one of them, grabbing for the package. Sam leaped to one side and dashed into the road. There was a screech of breaks and a car shuddered to a halt just in front of Sam. A policeman stepped out and then another. Sam glanced back at the phone box. But there was no one there – only the door swinging in the breeze…

Practising writing action sentences

Find examples in the story on pages 37–38 and create several of your own.

1 Use short sentences for dramatic tension.

They ran.

He screamed.

She jumped.

2 Use a 'But' sentence to add impact.

But they were trapped.

But she was caught.

But the door was locked.

3 Describe what happens – use powerful verbs of action.

His footsteps thudded on the road.

He spun round and grabbed the man.

Somebody seized her.

4 Describe sounds to make it seem real.

Footsteps pounded behind him.

He could hear their shouts.

The car slammed on its brakes.

5 Use sentence of 3 to build up the action.

He leaped over the fence, rolled down the slope and crashed into the wall.

She ducked down, held her breath and waited.

Write an extract from an adventure story in which someone is being chased. The main character sees a bicycle, jumps on and rides down a hill. Write the paragraph describing the bike ride. Think about what it would feel like, and use your senses to bring the action alive. Begin and end the paragraph like this:

Sam grabbed the bicycle and leaped on...

...he jumped off the bike and began to climb the wall.

Write a further extract from the same story, in which Sam now climbs up a drainpipe and scrambles through a window. He is still being chased! Begin and end the paragraph like this:

Without thinking, he grabbed the drain pipe and pulled himself up...

...he flopped onto the floor and looked around.

WRITING TIPS

Writing action paragraphs

To create realistic and exciting action, try using these techniques:

▶ Try to see the action in your mind.

▶ Do not have too much happening.

▶ Slow the pace when you write the action section so that your mind can concentrate on constructing the sentences and not get too caught up in the tangle of events!

▶ Describe what happens – use powerful verbs of action, e.g. *grab, grip, grasp, squeeze, punch, thud, thump, break, snap, crack, slap, dash, rush, jump, leap, swing, tug, pull, stagger, hurtle, shove, scratch, scrape.*

▶ Describe sounds to make it seem real, e.g. *snap, crack, scream, screech, yell, moan, groan, gasp, whisper, pound, blast, bellow, growl, howl.*

▶ Use suspense words such as *suddenly, without warning, at that moment, without hesitation.*

▶ Use short sentences to build up dramatic tension, e.g. *She jumped.*

▶ Use exclamations for punchy impact – *They ran!*

▶ Occasionally break the sentence rule by using a fragment for impact, e.g. *They were coming closer. Closer.*

▶ Use a 'But' sentence to add impact, e.g. *But there was no door!*

▶ Use sentence of 3 to build up the action, e.g. *Sam ran down the bank, leaped over the stream and landed with a thud.*

SHORT TASKS

1 Write the first two or three paragraphs of a story which starts with a character over-hearing something.

2 Write the opening two or three paragraphs of a story which starts with a character finding a secret message.

LONG TASKS

1 Write an adventure story that involves:
- a mysterious package;
- a journey;
- someone having to hide;
- a chase.

2 Write an adventure story:
- that begins with the main character exploring somewhere forbidden;
- the main character finds something precious;
- the main character gets imprisoned;
- the main character has to escape.

The body

"That was a good win," Tom said as he and Matt ran out of the school gate after the match against St. John's Primary.

"Mmm," agreed his friend, busy wrapping his Manchester United scarf round his neck to keep out the biting cold of the winter afternoon.

"Is your brother going to take you to that fair tonight?" Matt asked, when he was as warm as he was likely to be.

"Hope so," Tom replied, "but he's such an idiot. Who knows what he'll be doing by the time I get home!"

The boys turned left and walked up the High Street, brightly illuminated now in the deepening gloom.

"You got any sweets?" Tom asked, a few minutes later.

Matt dug deep into his bag and pulled out a packet, matted with bits of fluff and dust. Munching happily and re-living every moment of their recent success, the boys walked on towards their estate on the other side of town. Shops were beginning to shut and fewer people were about.

"Come on," suggested Matt, "let's cut through here – it'll take us to the park. I'm **really** starving. Wish I'd said Mum could come and get us now."

They turned into a dark, narrow alley, lined with dustbins. A truck was parked at the end. Two men were opening the tailgate. Something about them made the boys stop. As they watched, the men carefully lifted down a long shape wrapped in some kind of woollen material.

"Let's get him in, then," said one of the men.

Horrified, Tom turned to his friend. "**Him**!" he whispered. "They've got a body there, Matt! What'll we do?"

But Matt was still staring with his mouth open and said nothing as Tom began to creep through the shadows, keeping well out of sight.

"BOY CATCHES MURDERERS SINGLE-HANDED!" Tom muttered to himself, remembering Petie Burkis who talked in newspaper headlines in the class book 'The Midnight Fox'. He grinned at the thought of becoming a hero. "This'll be easy. I'll watch where they go and then call the police. Game over!"

The men, struggling under the weight of their load, disappeared through a door and into a building Tom did not recognise. They did not close the door. Tom inched forward into the darkness, confident that he would be able to give the police clear details. Ahead of him, he saw the men enter a brightly lit room.

Suddenly, something brushed Tom's face. He froze. Someone was next to him. Someone he couldn't see. There was a sound – a shuffle – nothing more. Did they know he was here? The wind whistled sharp as a dagger through the open door, sending icy shivers down his spine. He was about to be caught by vicious murderers! His heart raced. The light inside the building snapped off. Hardly daring to breath, Tom peered into the murky shadows. Something creaked. Gripping his bag tightly, Tom turned to run but someone had grabbed his ankle and he found himself face down on concrete…

… with a torch shining in his face.

"What are you doing, laddie?" a man asked. "This isn't the entrance, you know. Anyway, we're shut until tomorrow morning."

Tom looked dazed and turned to Matt who had arrived on the scene. Entrance? Closed? What did the man mean? Where were the murderers? Where was the body?

"This is the back of the museum, boys," the man repeated. "The entrance is on Park Street. This is the delivery area. We've just taken in something for our African exhibition and…"

"What?" Tom interrupted. "Like a dead body wrapped in cloth?"

The museum guard laughed. "A body? Well yes, I suppose so, but not a dead one! It's a statue made of wood – beautifully painted, it is. I thought I heard something – thought someone was trying to get in. You can't be too careful with so many treasures about."

Tom cast an embarrassed glance in Matt's direction. Talk about letting your imagination run away with you!

"Sorry to have disturbed you," he muttered. "We need to get home now. Bye!"

"Bye, lads. Come back and see your body tomorrow," he laughed. "Sorry to have scared you!"

The boys left the building and turned for home.

"So what about that last goal, then," Matt said. "Wasn't that a beauty!"

Start the sentence

Try using the sentence starts below to write your own sentences. The next word in each of the sentences could be the name of your character. Some could be short sentences and others could be longer ones.

When you have written your sentence, try turning it around and putting the sentence start later in the sentence. Discuss with your partner what difference it makes to a scary sentence.

Hardly daring to breathe, …

Without warning, …

Without turning back, …

Horrified, …

Silently, …

Suddenly, …

Shaking with fear, …

Trying to stop himself from shaking, …

Scary description

THINGS TO REMEMBER

SIMILES say that something is **like** something else.
The shadow slipped quick as a knife…

METAPHORS say that something is something else.
The darkness was a tunnel…

PERSONIFICATION makes an object seem human either by the way it looks or the way it behaves.
The wind moaned in the trees.

ALLITERATION uses a repeated sound for effect.
The shadows shivered…

Now try to use these powerful verbs in sentences with some different kinds of description. Try a mixture of short and longer sentences.

Gaped

Slid

Shivered

Groaned

Hissed

Slithered

Whispered

Clutched

Scratched

PRACTICE ACTIVITY ②

Agony Aunt

Sarah has just started to write suspense. She has remembered some of the advice but needs some help to improve. Work with a partner and make some notes about what is good and not so good about the writing. Then you can work together to try to improve it.

Suddenly the key turned in the lock. Ben turned around. He felt scared. Someone was outside. Someone had locked him in. He saw a shadow move past the door. It went very quickly. Inside the room was very dark. Ben shivered. What could it be?

WRITING TIPS

- ▶ Use short sentences for dramatic effect.
- ▶ Use questions to draw in the reader.
- ▶ Use exclamations for punch!
- ▶ Vary sentence length.
- ▶ Use longer sentences to hide the monster or build up tension, bit by bit.
- ▶ Hide the monster by using empty words such as 'something' or 'it'.
- ▶ Use powerful verbs.
- ▶ Use similes to build up the picture.
- ▶ Use personification to help create atmosphere.
- ▶ Use alliteration to make sentences memorable, e.g. *the snake slithered…*
- ▶ Use sounds to scare the reader, e.g. *something scratched on the window.*
- ▶ Use vague glimpses to build tension, e.g. *a shadow shifted…*
- ▶ Show how the character involved feels by describing their reaction, e.g. *he froze, grabbing the bag he…*
- ▶ Introduce darkness.
- ▶ Introduce the cold.
- ▶ If you get stuck, introduce something unexpected, e.g. *at that moment the bomb exploded*, or bring in a new character, or a new event, e.g. *a phone ringing, a knock at the door*, etc.
- ▶ Use a stock suspense tactic, e.g. *curtains moving in the wind, dark clouds, mist, feet on gravel, a whisper in the dark, rustling sounds…*

SHORT TASKS

1 HOME ALONE

Kelly is alone in her house for the first time at night. She has watched TV, phoned her friend and was about to go to bed when she heard an odd noise in the attic. She climbed the ladder to look inside.

Write a paragraph of suspense and another paragraph to continue the story. DO NOT FINISH IT.

2 THE OLD BARN

Two children are out playing. It starts to rain and they decide to go inside an old barn which is nearby.

Write a paragraph of suspense and another paragraph to continue the story. DO NOT FINISH IT.

Begin like this:

Without warning, the heavy wooden door slammed behind them...

LONG TASKS

1 MYSTERY IN THE CHURCHYARD

Write a story which contains a section of suspense.

You need to think about:
- Who your characters are – why are they in the churchyard?
- What happens in the churchyard to create suspense?
- What happens in the end?

2 FOOTSTEPS IN THE NIGHT

Write a story which contains a section of suspense.

You need to think about:
- Who your characters are – why are they out at night?
- What happens to create suspense?
- What happens in the end?

A Time Slip Story

Nick's history project

"So, what was it like inside an air-raid shelter, Grandma?" Nick asked, desperately trying to drag the conversation back to the information he needed for his history project.

"Well now, …quite cosy actually. We had it all fitted out. Oh! I've just remembered. You'll be interested in this."

Nick sighed as Grandma padded out of the room in her enormous fluffy blue slippers. This was the trouble with the older generation. Everything took ages! Didn't she understand he had to hand the work in tomorrow!

When Grandma returned, she was smiling. "This will help you, love," she said. "You can take some of it into school if you take great care. Look!" She opened a box and brought out some tatty books, a few puzzles, lots of old clothes… and a gas mask.

"Wow!" exclaimed Nick, seizing this last object. "That's great! Can I try it on?"

"It's not a good idea…" Grandma's voice faded as a high-pitched whining sound filled the air. Nick smelt burning. There was a scream. What was going on?

Pulling the mask off, Nick gaped in horror and disbelief at the scene. He was standing on the edge of a smouldering crater filled with shattered house bricks, bent pipes and pieces of broken furniture. Turning first to his left, Nick saw houses — not like in his street, or on Grandma's new estate, but like the old ones his other Grandma lived in. A fireman was sending a useless spray of water from a single hosepipe at one house as smoke billowed from upstairs windows and flames engulfed the inside. Suddenly, Nick was aware of the whining noise again. Of course — the air-raid siren! Everyone must be in the shelter. Turning the other way, Nick saw that there was less damage. An old-fashioned red telephone box caught his eye and then he noticed the cars. The glass in the windows was smashed but he could still recognise the types — just like the ones in his Classic Cars Top Trumps Pack.

Before Nick had time to consider the impossibility of his situation, a faint cry from behind made him swing round. There was rubble in that direction as far as the eye could see. Then came the cry again — but more urgently. Testing the ground carefully, Nick followed the noise and came to a partly demolished house. A young girl was lying on what remained of a sitting room floor, with a ceiling rafter trapping her leg.

Without hesitating, Nick rushed over.

"Don't worry," he said confidently. "I'll get you out. Does your leg hurt?"

"Not really," she replied. "I'm just stuck. But that's going to come down in a minute," she added pointing at the other side of the building. "Please, help quickly!"

Nick bent down and carefully shifted the wooden beam a little. There was a sickening crack as he dislodged other pieces of masonry in the room. He tried again and this time moved it enough for the girl to wriggle out.

"Thank you ever so much!" she exclaimed. "I went back inside for Susie, my doll. I couldn't leave her. They must have all thought I was following to the shelter. What's your name? I'm Maggie."

"Nick. Here let me help you find them."

At that moment, a man dashed past. "What are you two doing?" he yelled. "Why aren't you in the shelter? Put on your masks now and come with me."

Nick fumbled with unfamiliar straps and placed the gas mask over his head. The whirring stopped. The smell disappeared.

"… to put them on, you know," Grandma's voice was saying. "Funny smells."

Nick snatched the mask off and gaped. "Grandma!" he shouted. "It's you!"

"Well, who did you think it was, silly!" she said in surprise. "You putting that on really took me back," Grandma continued. "I had a friend when we lived in London — Maggie was her name. She got caught in the blitz. We were all so worried for a bit."

"Yes, but she got out," said Nick without thinking. "She only went back for her doll."

"Yes, but how did you know that?" Grandma asked curiously.

"Oh you must have mentioned it before," Nick said quickly, "when you were telling me that you weren't an evacuee like lots of children." Grandma frowned as if trying to remember. "Listen, Grandma," Nick hurried on, "I really must go. You've helped ever such a lot. I reckon I'm going to do the best history project ever."

Brainstorm with a friend

Think about settings in the past.

You might choose something you've studied in history or something you've read about or seen on a film.

Work with a partner or a small group and BRAINSTORM useful precise words and phrases that could help bring the setting to life.

Use a thesaurus to help.

Here are some ideas to get you started:

- a London street, 100 years ago, 50 years ago, last year;
- a workhouse (think of "Oliver Twist");
- the home of an elderly relative;
- a setting you know well – for example, somewhere that you go on holiday – but with some changes;
- a Roman fort on Hadrian's Wall – centurions are preparing for an attack by the Picts;
- on board a ship with one of the Tudor explorers.

Remember to think about the senses – what you SEE, what you HEAR, what you SMELL.

Agony Aunt

In this story, Sam was in his bedroom reading a book. The pages began to whirl around and the time slip happened. This was a good idea, but the writer did not describe the new setting very clearly.

Sam looked around in surprise. He wasn't at home any more. He was in the street and the houses were different from the houses in his street. The people looked different as well. Sam didn't know where he was so he thought he'd ask someone.

Work with a partner to help this writer.

Think about:
• any sentences you might keep;
• any sentences to change;
• any new sentences you may need to write;
• the advice you might give about the last sentence.

WRITING TIPS

▶ Try to see the setting in your mind.

▶ When creating settings, use specific detail.

▶ Think about what you can see and hear.

▶ Add in what time of day it is.

▶ Think about the weather.

▶ Use the setting to create atmosphere, and manipulate the reader's feelings. For instance, a lane on a hot sunny day is one thing but the same lane on a dark wintry night feels scary!

▶ If writing about another time, research the period.

▶ Look at photos or paintings and note details. Use the details in your writing.

▶ Use a few solid facts about the past to make the setting seem real.

▶ Invent some extra details of your own – make sure they seem to fit in with the time.

 **SHORT TASKS**

1 A REAL TRIP

Kelly is in the library searching for some information for a school project.

Write the first two sections of the time slip story.

The opening will be set in the library or museum.

The build-up will be set in a time of your choice. It can be a long time ago or in the recent past. You choose.

You must move Kelly into the new time and write a precise description of her new setting.

2 GRANDMOTHER'S GARDEN

Mitchell is visiting his Grandmother, who has a well kept garden. While he is playing, he falls off the swing and feels dizzy. When he opens his eyes, the garden is different.

Write the build up to this story starting like this:

When the dizziness passed, Mitchell opened his eyes – and stared.

You need to continue this section of the story but also concentrate on DESCRIBING the new garden.

LONG TASKS

1 ALICE TO THE RESCUE!

Write a story about Alice, who goes into the past and helps someone.

You need to think about:
- where Alice is at the start of the story;
- how she gets into the past;
- who she helps and how she helps them;
- how she gets home;
- how to end the story.

2 I'M ROMAN, TRAIL ME!

Write a time slip story in which a child from the past (this could be Tudor, Greek, Roman, etc) suddenly appears in the present and meets a lonely child. Tell the story from the point of view of the child from the past.

You need to think about:
- where the child appears;
- who they meet;
- what happens;
- how she/he gets home;
- how to end the tale.

JOURNEY TO SOMEWHERE

SCENE 1: *inside a small spacecraft. The craft has crashed and is stuck nose first in the ground. Lights on the instrument panel are flashing wildly. Smoke is pouring out of a grill. Two young teenage boys are lying on the floor.*

GREG: Are you OK? *(Gets off the floor and rubs his head. There is a little blood on his hand.)*

WILL: I think so… Where are we?

GREG: Dunno. Exciting isn't it!

WILL: No! How can you say that! No-one knows we're here anyway. It was a daft idea to take the exploration pod without asking!

GREG: *(laughs)* Well, I couldn't ask, could I! They wouldn't 've let me!

WILL: Yeah – and we know why! You have NO IDEA what you're doing! No-one knows we're here and we could be on a dangerous planet!

GREG: **Not** very likely considering the number of perfectly harmless planets that have been found so far! And for your information, I know perfectly well how to fly this thing. There was a surge in the plasma injection unit – but I wouldn't expect **you** to understand that. It couldn't be helped.

WILL: *(mutters under his breath)* I bet my Dad would've known what to do. Well, what do we do? Those lights shouldn't be flashing should they?

The boys move over to the control panel and Greg starts pushing buttons. Will goes to the look-out window – then turns away and slumps down onto the floor.

WILL: I don't like this AT ALL! You're not making it better. We're going to be stuck here AND we'll be in SO much trouble!

GREG: Well. One or the other, certainly. If we're stuck here, they won't find us, so we **won't** be in trouble! *(He laughs at the horrified look on Will's face.)* Oh, **do** grow up! It's exciting! Come on. *(Goes over to Will and pulls him up.)* Let's go and explore. It's OK, the atmosphere's breathable – I checked with the computer.

The boys move towards the hatch – Will very reluctantly. Greg presses a button, the hatch opens and they leave the spacecraft.

SCENE 2: *outside the spacecraft. The land is covered with boulders and a few purple plants with spiky leaves grow in clumps. A grey mist swirls a few metres above the ground.*

WILL: Ohh... This is creepy. That mist! Are you **sure** the air is OK? *(puts his hand in front of his mouth and nose)*

GREG: I said so, didn't I? I'm going this way. *(He moves to the left towards a higher group of boulders.)*

WILL: Don't leave me behind. I don't like this!

A metallic sound comes from behind the boulder.

What's that?

GREG: What? I didn't hear anything.

WILL: Listen.

The boys stop. The sound comes again – louder.

GREG: I don't know. Do you want to look?

WILL: No I don't! I didn't want to go outside in the first place. This isn't fun. It's stupid!

GREG: Yeah – but it'll make a great story back at the space station!

Suddenly, a flash of light leaps from right to left. It lands in a clump of purple plants. The leaves start to move in a menacing fashion.

On second thoughts… *(grabs Will and starts to run)* We can always make it up! Come on!

They race back to the hatch of the spacecraft.

We need to get this thing going again. Let's open the communication channel. Suddenly, I rather like the idea of getting into trouble with your Dad.

The boys enter the spacecraft.

Agony Aunt

Read this section from a play:

SCENE: *at the base of a cliff at the seaside*

Boy: Help!

Girl: Where are you? I can't see you!

Boy: I'm over here – on the ground.

Girl: What happened?

Boy: I was climbing up and I slipped.

Girl: That's stupid. It says not to on that notice.

Boy: Yeah, well! I know why now, don't I! My leg hurts.

Girl: Is it broken?

Boy: I don't know. I hope not but it hurts like hell! Have you got a mobile?

Girl: Yes. Don't worry. I'll ring for an ambulance.

The writer has not included any stage directions or character directions. This means we don't have much idea about what the boy and girl do or how they speak. This means that we don't know about their characters.

Work with a partner and work out what you would add to improve the scene. Do not add in too many instructions.

Try acting it out by following your own directions. Was it better?

From story to play

Think about some short stories you know really well. Fairy tales are good for this activity – or even nursery rhymes!

Take a small section of the story and work with a partner or small group to turn it into a play.

IDEAS:

• The part in "Cinderella" when the ugly sisters try on the glass slipper.

• The scene in "Little Red Riding Hood" when the wolf visits Grandma.

• The scene in the town as Humpty Dumpty fell off the wall!

Each of you should take a character. Work together to write a short scene.

Your aim is to show the characters clearly through what they say and the way they say their words.

Try acting it out. Were you successful?

WRITING TIPS

▶ Put stage directions in brackets – keep them to a minimum.

▶ Start each new speech on a new line.

▶ You do not need speech marks or the word 'said'.

▶ Do not have too many characters – 2 or 3 will do.

▶ Try to find ways to make your characters distinctive – by how they speak and the things they say – give one a typical saying to repeat.

▶ Think about the types they are, e.g. bossy, shy, aggressive…

▶ Think about how they feel, e.g. sad, lonely, angry…

▶ Make sure that what they say reflects how they feel or the type of character that they are.

▶ When writing, say the speech out loud to see how it sounds.

▶ Keep the plot simple.

▶ Use the dialogue to move the plot forwards.

▶ Use the narrator sparingly to:
  • set the scene, e.g. *The play opens in a modern classroom.*
  • move action forwards, e.g. *A burglar climbs in through the window.*
  • describe a character, e.g. *The man is tall, thin and wears a dark coat.*
  • offer a view, e.g. *He looks in pain.*

1 I WANT TO PLAY FOOTBALL

Derin wants to go out and play football with his friends.

His Mum and Dad want him to go and do his homework first.

Write a conversation between them IN THE FORM OF A PLAY in which Derin tries to PERSUADE his parents to let him go out.

Finish the scene when:
• either Derin goes outside;
• or Derin goes to do his homework.

2 THE BULLIES

Scene: a school playground.

David and Jake have just crossed the playground to find Ben, a boy in their class, whom they enjoy upsetting.

Write a short scene between them. Start like this:

David: *Oh, look who it is! All alone then are you, Ben!*

LONG TASKS

1 Two children are enjoying playing in a deserted house on the edge of their village, even though they know they should not be there. It's beginning to get dark. Suddenly they hear noises.

Write the rest of the scene from this point until they leave the house.

You should think about:
• what they hear/see;
• who or what it is;
• what happens.

2 AN INTERVIEW

You work for a local radio station and have been asked to find a guest star for the next show.

Write down the interview you have.

Think about:
• the questions you will ask;
• how you will show why you and your guest spoke;
• how you will begin and end the interview.

Badger Publishing Limited
26 Wedgwood Way, Pin Green Industrial Estate,
Stevenage, Hertfordshire SG1 4QF
Telephone: 01438 356907
Fax: 01438 747015
www.badger-publishing.co.uk
enquiries@badger-publishing.co.uk

Badger Test Revision Guides
Key Stage 2 English – Writing Fiction
ISBN 1 85880 360 8

Text © Pie Corbett & Ann Webley 2003
Complete work © Badger Publishing Limited 2003

Publisher: David Jamieson
Editor: Paul Martin
Designed by Lodestone Publishing Limited; www.lodestonepublishing.com
Illustrations by Fred van Deelen

Printed in the UK.